Animals That Live in the Grasslands

MeerKats

By Therese Harasymiw

Gareth Stevens
Publishing

Please visit our Web site, www.garethstevens.com. For a free color catalog of all our high-quality books, call toll free 1-800-542-2595 or fax 1-877-542-2596.

Library of Congress Cataloging-in-Publication Data

Harasymiw, Therese.
 Meerkats / Therese Harasymiw.
     p. cm. – (Animals that live in the grasslands)
Includes index.
ISBN 978-1-4339-3876-4 (pbk.)
ISBN 978-1-4339-3877-1 (6-pack)
ISBN 978-1-4339-3875-7 (library binding)
1. Meerkat–Juvenile literature. 2. Grassland animals–Juvenile literature. I. Title.
QL737.C235H36 2011
599.74'2–dc22

                                            2010000406

First Edition

Published in 2011 by
Gareth Stevens Publishing
111 East 14th Street, Suite 349
New York, NY 10003

Designer: Michael J. Flynn
Editor: Therese Shea

Photo credits: Cover, pp. 1, 5, 7, 9, 11, 13, 15, 19, 21, back cover Shutterstock.com; p. 17 Mattias Klum/National Geographic/Getty Images.

Printed in the United States of America

CPSIA compliance information: Batch #CS10GS: For further information contact Gareth Stevens, New York, New York at 1-800-542-2595.

Table of Contents

Boldface words appear in the glossary.

Meet the Meerkats

Meerkats are small, furry animals. They are around 10 inches (25 cm) tall when they stand. Meerkats live in the **grasslands**, plains, and deserts of southern Africa.

A meerkat is usually gray, brown, or tan. It has dark bands of color on its back. It has dark circles around its eyes, too. Its long, thin tail has a black tip.

dark circle

dark bands
of color

black tip

Pack Animals

Meerkats live in packs. A pack may have as many as 30 meerkats. Packs sometimes fight each other. Meerkats in big packs help keep each other safe.

Meerkat packs live under the ground in **burrows**. Each home has many **entrances**, tunnels, and rooms. Meerkats sleep in burrows. They also use them to hide from the sun's heat.

burrow

Feeding Time

Each morning, meerkats leave their burrows to look for food. Meerkats mainly eat bugs. They also eat spiders, lizards, birds, and snakes. Meerkats have large front claws that help them dig for food.

claws

Some animals like to eat meerkats. Meerkat enemies include **jackals**, hawks, and eagles. One meerkat in the pack watches for enemies. It stands guard on its back legs as the others dig for food.

Meerkats take turns being the guard after they have eaten. If the meerkat guard sees a **predator**, it makes a special noise. Then, the other meerkats run for cover or attack as a pack.

Meerkat Pups

In each pack, only a few meerkats have babies each year. Meerkat pups leave the burrows when they are 4 or 5 weeks old. "Babysitter" meerkats help parents care for pups.

pup

When there is danger, meerkats may cover pups with their bodies. When the pups are older, they help other meerkats. Working together helps meerkats stay alive!

Fast Facts

Height	about 10 inches (25 centimeters) standing up
Length	about 18 inches (46 centimeters) from head to tip of tail
Weight	about 2 pounds (1 kilogram)
Diet	bugs, spiders, lizards, birds, and snakes
Average life span	about 12 years in the wild

Glossary

burrow: a hole or tunnel dug by an animal as a living space

entrance: an opening

grasslands: land on which grass is the main kind of plant life

jackal: an African animal that looks like a bushy-tailed dog

predator: an animal that hunts, kills, and eats other animals as food

For More Information

Books

Clutton-Brock, Tim. *Meerkat Manor: Flower of the Kalahari.* New York: Simon & Schuster, 2007.

Storad, Conrad J. *Meerkats.* Minneapolis, MN: Lerner Publications, 2007.

Web Sites

Animal Diversity Web

animaldiversity.ummz.umich.edu/site/accounts/ information/Suricata_suricatta.html
Read about the life of meerkats and see photos of meerkats in the wild.

National Geographic: Meerkat

nationalgeographic.com/animals/mammals/meerkat.html
Print a sheet of meerkat facts and see a video of a meerkat and one of its enemies.

Index

About the Author

After several months of studying a pack of meerkats in their natural environs, author and editor Therese Harasymiw collaborated with naturalist and professional art designer Michael Flynn in creating a book to share these animals with a young audience. The author and designer work in Buffalo, New York.